Blight Summer

poems by

Margaret Young

Finishing Line Press
Georgetown, Kentucky

Blight Summer

ACKNOWLEDGMENTS

These poems first appeared in the following:

"Rounds" in *Zigzag Folios*
"Ipswich" published as "Essex County" in *Boston and Beyond* poetry blog
"New House, September" in *Borderlands*
"Lullaby," "Still Life, Landscape, Snapshot," "San Fruttoso," "Sestri Levante,"
"Fresh Thoughts, Cove Park" in earlier versions online, Tupelo Press 30/30
project
"Sestri Levante" in *Like One—Poems for Boston* anthology
"First Day of Teaching After Maternity Leave" in *Mom Egg Review*
"Baby Loves Trucks" in *Literary Mama*
"Blight Summer" in *Muddy River Review*
"Lullaby" in *Extracts: Daily Dose of Lit* blog
"Moving On" and "September Diary, Dreams and Walking" in *Superstition
Review*

Publisher: Leah Maines

Editor: Christen Kincaid

Cover Art: ©Paul Cary Goldberg, www.paulcarygoldberg.com

Author Photo: Jeff Heyer / Deeper Still Photography

Cover Design: Elizabeth Maines McCleavy

Printed in the USA on acid-free paper.
Order online: www.finishinglinepress.com
            also available on amazon.com

Author inquiries and mail orders:
Finishing Line Press
P. O. Box 1626
Georgetown, Kentucky 40324
U. S. A.

Table of Contents

For Quentin,
of course

New House, September

The neighbor boy, Mason
the stone-lifter, bounds into our garden,
touches sculpture. That one's clay,
kid, like plates, like us. We learn
these tongues together, math
of thriving, art and artist,
flame and origin—
there goes our truck for cans
and boxes, bottles rattling
towards their shattering.

Rounds

The dogs of Beverly are perfect
buttered toast magazine gloss
hounds and terriers.

At Dane Beach someone's already
arranged blue mussel shells into rosettes.
Just like you dreamed it.

Babies are strapped down,
heads filled with sky,
rolling along the shore
more or less merrily.

Your namesake hurricane is coming. Soon.

Linguistic Inventory at 20 Months

Tail and cat,
moon and tomato.

Dad, clock,
tick tock, hee haw.

Pig's snort, fish's splash,
same splash for a seashell, for a drink

of water. Dig dig, roll roll, siren's
squeal, truck and car, oh you know car,

and ca for birds because of all
the graveyard crows, both

pronounced the same like
you're a Boston native, *cah*.

September Diary, Dreams and Walking

Grace looks odd spelled out, like it should be graze, maybe, or thanks in Spanish, or that town in France that makes perfume. Outside the window where the baby naps, a forklift rumbles, beeps, aligns itself with a short stack of long boards.

Real hubbard squashes, but the dream put smiley faces on their gray-blue, toad-bumpy surfaces.

Blue heron standing in the artificial pond at work today. Sometimes I'd like to fold up into myself like that.

Are there rationalist goths, we asked, passing a clump of painted kids in Salem, near the witchy stores. There were abundant greyhounds, loose groups of grownups pushing a lone stroller.

I dream my mother, gone twenty-three years. Just there, jumbled in with everyone.

Sing willow, sing sycamore, poke poke berries turning black and luscious. Low clouds scuttling out to sea, wind tossing it all around.

Score a bar of baking chocolate, block of bittersweet, hunk of dark breaks into daylight. Ice forming on the dashboard. One milk mushroom, one milk song: the baby ate my voice. I'll rise again, maybe next week.

Lullaby

Drive west with me.
Night falling in the jungle
night falling on the ocean
falling on the children of beasts.

Remember when we drove
over the cliff into the tunnel,
along the path scattered
by the yellow moon?

Do you remember how new
we were, do you remember
ocean animals on YouTube,
souls along the bare shore?

The couple dances in the jungle,
in the parking lot, they drink oil,
lap love like gravy, night falling
on their lips, on the hoods of cars.

Ipswich

Snow moon rises, not in
happiness nor sorrow but
moon mood, circle circle.

The stairs crossing the dunes
at Crane Beach have poems carved on them,
short lines about tides and terns,

returns. You drag your dark cloud
like a wet sack, past the unexpected seal

> come onshore maybe to study
> all the two-legs, hairy four-legs,
> some roped and saddled, tails streaming

> or maybe just trying to nap,
> but why lift head then tail,
> slowly, each ten seconds or so?

Small children in bright coats stop.
Parents move them gently on.

Motif #2

A harbor's horizontals, rose/turquoise light of change-time, creep of gold and white through air, water and sand. Mooring ropes stretch and sag, some diagonal relief. Mast, flagpole, smokestack, cloud-streak.

Here at the shore we sigh, look at our feet and back out at the sea. The water wants to kiss us, no, it wants to kill us, no, it wants to lap lap and say nothing. We dump our longings on the shore and let them drift. Alongshore, we tie our hopes to rocks, we lash our platitudes.

The painter was sleepy, all those dawns. Why not a sunset, said the landlord. But the light's all crooked then.

No, No

we don't talk don't write about
family so much, live ones at least

we are too shy they are too close
breath clouding phone receivers

cheeks greasing tiny screens
we squirm at such directness

it's flat and sour, twanging
like the summer rental's upright

only a few notes sound
unbearable still we don't
want to go finding out which

but sometimes it's *fun*
a nephew demonstrates
(bang key, jump back theatrically)

and some just like grating their souls
on lumps of pain, I tell the pigtailed
poet at my sister's bridal brunch.

My Stepsister's

wedding cupcakes: white cake
baked (scratch) by bridesmaids,
brothers in the seaside rental. Frosted,
sprinkled, boxed and stacked where

ants found them, tiny black ants
swarmed white buttercream,
feasted on greenblue sugar
on my sister's wedding day so

her surgeon father picked them off,
killed each ant with love, her quiet
father smoothed white frosting
and we who knew stayed smooth

with that secret, hours
later, we smiled,
bit in.

Moving On

is more than north American self-helpishness
but ancient inevitable, letting water
for instance go the way it knows.

Glaciers melt, bears roam the woods
where my sister runs, I run Bear Creek
with my blond dog, only one heron
between here and Gustine, it is not
my mother.

Put the flat of your knife on the garlic
clove and slam your fist down, pretend it's
your ex, the TV chef suggests. How about
a demon of your own creation?

I want to hit my brother.

He's neither bear nor evil,
just born under a crusty sign.

And my mother is a cypress, a coyote,
and my father wrote a poem
about chopping garlic for us all.

Lesson Plan

Pick up a green and yellow orange.
Its curve, your curled fingers.
The table of envelopes recedes.

Where a stone trestle crosses
the creek: someone dropped
a mirror to contain
fragments of sky and branches.

Yesterday you jumped, umbrella broken,
across two lanes of leaves, hailed
a squirrel skidding the wires above.
Today you build a shrine,
twist-ties and bendy straws.

Civilization

Beethoven's seventh sounds
like Western optimism, nature soul
swelling Romantic, Austrian strings to
Bacchic clarinets, the one four
five four one of syntax, synthesis
and flow into the second movement, pure Pan

great if you like your rivers rock-filled
so the water roars, whitens the land
with splash then rolls to calm again
and then a theme, chorus, cadence, hush

and here's that rhythm again
and Ludwig's also now this mutt
on our rug, hair like a rope mop,
our friend Lana's looking after him
for friends of hers, composers, she has
to pick a carcass from their freezer,
organic bird or rabbit, place it
and Ludwig in a room used
solely for that purpose: the dog
stalks it, pouncing on cold flesh,
shakes it around, insert here
reference to fast movement,
or nineteenth century slaughter
of subject people, or this
young century's hungers.

Flow Bit

Dig like backhoe
jump like fox
bend like branches
graveyard hemlocks,

copper beeches and the beach sand
is cold but soft and fluid,
studded with rocks and jetsam.

Gull, crab, gull, clam. Duck,
duck goose. With the wind
across the water go the boats,
nets ready, full of desire.

San Fruttoso

The town I missed—Portofino ferry stopped
there but the kid had fallen asleep, head in my lap
so we stayed on board with the three man/
one dog crew. They pulled out of the port
too small to dock in for an hour,
motored out to sea a little way, then
cut the engine.

While you visited the abbey,
tenth century walls, bones of holy men
I sat in shade, gazing at the coast,
blue glinting water while the radio played Fun.'s
"We Are Young," which you despise
but I smiled at, glad not to be setting
anything on fire that afternoon.

Next week in Genoa I toured a monastery
with hundreds of reliquaries and more hundreds
of tiny paintings to commemorate safe
return of ships, while you took him
to the aquarium, grand expensive tomb.

Sestri Levante

Across the peninsula from where Byron
swam (according to the plaque)

in a park one hotel away from the beach
(seashell fountains, small playgrounds)

flanked by bulky coin-op rides (helicopter,
dragon, mule with hat and jug of hooch)

there is this little carousel: monster truck,
princess coach, Formula One racecar

all chrome and glitter, airbrushed
unlicensed characters.

The operator takes our euro, smokes,
plays Snoop Dogg every time

we go there, "Gin and Juice"
another time a newer one,

something about bitches and hos as my son
and Italian kids ride circles, waving.

The sea is Dora Markus here, and Shelley.
We watch it snuff out one night's sun.

My son says he'll remember. What,
I ask. Everything, he says.

All Saints'

The earth, your mother, says—

you ask her. No, you.
                          Say we
go to Mexico, Oaxaca for example
where they make chocolate sacred,
bake sweet bread
for the dead, your mother
wants some.

The remembered
ones get fed.

By the Graveyard by the Sea

Crow calls high above the backhoe
digging a fresh pit right next to
last year's still-fresh rectangle.

Surfing is dance, too, arrested fall.
The ocean smells like cat food
says the black dog in the books,
the dogs are all going to that tree
over there, the words all going
to that hole in the ground.

The newborn seals (verb
for their birth is *pupping*)
fall through ice before
they've learned to swim.

Same seals, same babies, those white ones
we wrote letters to, I mean
for, in third grade.

Usufruct

I pick grapes from a chain link fence
around the corner, hand them over
my shoulder to the baby on my back, after
a few days not bothering to chew away seeds.

Tart green centers, sweet blue peels,
second ripening since we moved east.
I tell Quentin about pomegranates
from the blind alley near our California house;
the dog and I invariably had the whole block
to ourselves. There were grapefruits, too,
pistachios and some dusty green grapes
I often missed, but the pomegranates—
there were two kinds, one smaller and rounder,
a deeper red, sometimes I'd juice them.

A yard dog at the alley's corner always
ran its fenceline barking furiously
but after we passed him

there was silence, dust and lusty weeds,
the dog would walk under
ground-scraping branches and vines
so   slowly,
sniffing each rich inch, reading
rat scribbles, cat notes,
raccoon poems.

New House, June

Daylilies are peasants, orange gluts
of six-part petals lolling,
fighting for light and water
between lilac and pokeweed.

Outside purple walls and double panes,
lightning's discreet and distant,
lightning and rain and more
glad bells.

Baby Loves Trucks

Treaded treasure palaces,
trailers pulling pleasure
pomps of dig and carry.

Let's all get overrolled
by oil tankers, grinding barrel-
bellies of concrete, trash.

Open door, climb in the back
nestle in pallets cozy as boxcars
or climb the tractor's throne:

pull gears shift blades
push buckets into earth
dig in, lift up.

Memo

Don't put that away it's art,
part of the installation
we make each moment.

The orange bead, the blue whale
finger puppet, ivy curling from its vase,
the rolling pin, bentwood rocker with out-sticking nails,
lightly snoring dog, the new cat,
some lessons are about the dark,
some are about piedness,
red gold black, in this cat-case.

First Day of Teaching after Maternity Leave

Milk vomit on black velvet
looks like a galaxy,

the one we live in,
named for milk.

Two Raspberry Moons

1. *Connors Farm*

A green frog leaps
behind the ice cream freezer.

The alpaca needs a shave.
Loosestrife chokes blueberries,
proud old shrubs.

Orange lily   yellow lily
yellow tractor   green truck.

2. *Brooksby Farm*

Past highway, mall, mall to reach
these pigs browsing their rain-damp pens.

Short trees climb obedient rows,
peaches sink into their slatty boxes.

If time's a pomegranate, space might be
more mushroom, worm-holy, spinning
matter out of rot.

High Tide, Wind

He climbs the rock in fire engine boots
to splash in a puddle on top—

can't puddle-stomp in poems,
too cheap   way too much sweetness,
slick red rubber painted with headlight
eyes and wheels, man-machine
moment when foot is flow,
stomper and stomped-in, one.

Harvest Festival

Two parked tractors, open cab and closed cab, both wear forklifts. Friendly yellow caution signs all over. One knob on one tractor slides between two settings, turtle and rabbit. The giant lawnmower's for sitting too, leaping deer profiled on its steering wheel. A tall red hound runs through the parking lot—a deer, my son jokes. The emu tosses a tomato over its dinosaur head again and again, swallowing a bite each time. A pig stands up, half dipped in mud dark as black bean paste. Quentin next to the fence, leans in, says *I am taking care of these pigs*. The baby turkeys, dirty white rags, he tells a story. About a train.

Educational

1.

"Funkytown" playing inside the coffeeshop
and by the electric dancing turtle at the house
where I drop off my son. Won't you
take me to the river-mouth, the funky
harbor, Gloucester where the fish
are vanishing, won't you join the flow
of shiny cars in cold sunshine?

2.

No man is a sandwich. Don't eat books.
A is for apple, she is for cheese.
We are all one, I'm a hummingbird,
dancing backwards, sideways, I'm
a sunbeam, clogged with dust.
He calls for Mandelbrot set videos by name,
he wants to see Groovy, over and over.
S is for spiral, sickle, seek.

3.

We sing "America," Paul Simon's, in the car
going north to Canada, sing "This Land is Your
Land," paper placemats in the diner
tell how forestry benefits upstate New York,
there are painted sawblades on the wall,
leaping bass and seasons on the farm.

In Montreal we ride to the hotel's top,
the Gold Floor, twenty-one, with six
lamps flanking each room's door,
we ride the escalators down to parking,
down to subway, ride that too.

Fresh Thoughts, Cove Park

Where do we go when we die he asks (four,
red trike, cowboy hat). I tell him a few viewpoints,
get around to Orpheus, which gets us to the playground.

Cold wind off the ocean, an autistic boy
hugs our dog. I read Celan and don't slide
down slides, I'm in a skirt, I swing.

We load up purple pansies, yellow tulips.
White ladies at the greenhouse are sour, but
outside dandelions bloom, the stream runs fast

between its culverts, crows walk down the street
talking to themselves, and only the roadkill
rabbit's ears remain.

Blight Summer

Someone's invented
artificial fireflies;
they're cheaper.

No definite summer hit
but everywhere we hear
the dead man's beats,
remember his fierce dancing.

One storm never arrived, just pushed tides up,
dumped out seaweed. Geese all happy.

Back in the garden, a tomato falls.
These are the last ones, crowding
the counter, purple Russians, enormities,
titanics, mementos.

Margaret Young's poems and essays have appeared in *Cider Press Review, The Journal, Phoebe, Superstition Review,* and numerous other print and online journals. Her first poetry collection *Willow from the Willow* was chosen for Cleveland State University Poetry Center's Cleveland Poets series, and her second, *Almond Town,* won the Bright Hill Press Poetry Award. Young is translating the work of Argentine poet Débora Benacot, and her translation of Sergio Inestroza's *El espacio improbable de un haikú* has been published by Obsidiana press. She teaches writing and cultural studies at Endicott College and lives in Beverly, Massachusetts with her husband and son.